THE BENNETT SISTERS FRENCH COOKBOOK

Recipes inspired by the Series

LISE MCCLENDON

Thalia Press

CONTENTS

Explore all the author's works at
LiseMcClendon.com

OFF TO FRANCE

Chapter One

CASSOULET FOR TWO

*C*assoulet is a traditional peasant stew of Southwest France, named for the earthenware dish it is served in. There are regional differences but most cassoulets today include white beans, sausage, various other meats, and duck legs.

There is a tradition of keeping a huge stew going for days, or months, on a slow fire, but that isn't necessary to enjoy the rich flavors of the Languedoc. If you go to Carcassone, the magical walled town rumored to have inspired Cinderella's castle at Disneyland, be sure to try their cassoulet.

Ingredients

1 15 oz can of white beans

2 Toulouse or similar sausages

2 strips of pork belly (or uncured, unsmoked bacon or pancetta)

2 duck legs, cooked (confit)
1 onion, chopped
2 cloves of garlic, minced
bay leaf, sprig of thyme
1 tbsp tomato paste
Olive oil, butter or a little duck fat
A pint of chicken stock

Preparation:

In a cast iron pot heat 2 tbsp of olive oil with a tbsp of butter and/or duck fat then fry the sausages and pork. Remove the meat to a plate, then sauté the onions until soft.

Stir in the tomato paste and add the garlic, bay leaf, and thyme. Put the meat back in the pot (including the duck confit), add the beans, pour in enough chicken stock to cover.

Put the lid on and put the pot in a 300F oven for at least 1 hour, checking to keep ingredients moist. Stir and top up with stock as necessary. When the cassoulet is ready, the liquids should be absorbed but the ingredients coated with a creamy sauce. Generously season according to your taste, and put back in a hot oven, uncovered, for 10 – 20 minutes, until a crispy crust forms.

Pair the cassoulet with a robust red wine from Southwest France like a Cahors, Côteaux de Quercy or Corbières.

Chapter Two

HACHIS PARMENTIER

Hachis Parmentier is a meat-and-mashed-potato pie that is customarily made with leftovers from a boiled beef dinner, like pot-au-feu. If you have leftover beef and broth, you can use it.

As portrayed in **Odette and the Great Fear**, a famine spread throughout France and the wheat crop withered in the years before the French Revolution. The French weren't accustomed to eating potatoes, preferring bread. The dish is named after Antoine-Augustin Parmentier, a French pharmacist, nutritionist, and inventor who, in the late 18th century, was instrumental in the promotion of the potato as an edible crop. The word "*hachis*" means a dish in which the ingredients are chopped or minced, from the same root as the English word "hatchet."

Hachis Parmentier is made in three steps: the beef and broth (or leftovers), the filling made with sausage and tomato paste, and the mashed potato topping, similar to a cottage or shepherd's pie. The mashed potatoes require a food mill or potato ricer for best quality. Build the layers in a 2-quart casserole like a Pyrex dish, 10-inch or so, round or square.

Makes 4+ servings

Ingredients
The beef
(If you're using leftover beef stew, skip to the end of this section.)

1 pound cube steak or boneless beef chuck, cut into small pieces

1 small onion, sliced

1 small carrot, trimmed, peeled and cut into 1-inch-long pieces

1 small celery stalk, trimmed and cut into 1-inch-long pieces

2 garlic cloves, smashed and peeled

2 parsley sprigs

1 bay leaf

1 teaspoon salt

1/4 teaspoon black peppercorns

6 cups water

1/2 beef bouillon cube (optional)

The filling
1-1/2 tablespoons olive oil

1/2 pound sausage, sweet or spicy, removed from casings if necessary

1 teaspoon tomato paste

Salt and freshly ground pepper

. . .

The topping

    2 pounds russet potatoes, peeled and quartered

    1/2 cup whole milk

    1/4 cup heavy cream

    3 tablespoons unsalted butter, at room temperature, plus 1 tablespoon butter, cut into bits

    Salt and freshly ground pepper

    1/2 cup grated Gruyere, Comte, or Emmental

    2 tablespoons freshly grated Parmesan (optional)

The beef: Put all the ingredients except the bouillon cube in a heavy Dutch oven and bring to a boil, skimming off the foam and solids. Lower the heat, simmer for 1 1/2 hours. The broth will be mild. If you want it stronger, stir in the 1/2 bouillon cube.

Drain the meat, reserving the broth. Transfer the meat to a cutting board and discard the vegetables, or if they've still got some flavor, hold on to them for the filling. Traditionally *hachis Parmentier* has no vegetables but you can add them if you want. Strain the broth. (The beef and bouillon can be made up to one day ahead, covered and refrigerated.)

*If using leftover stew, strain it and cover broth and beef separately. Continue on from here.

Chop the beef into tiny pieces. You could do this in a food processor, but the texture will be better if chopped by hand.

. . .

The filling:

Butter the 2-quart casserole dish.

In a large skillet over medium, heat the olive oil. When it's hot, add the sausage, breaking up the clumps of meat, until the sausage is just pink. Add the beef and tomato paste and stir to mix. Add 1 cup of the broth, enough to moisten the filling, and bring to a boil. Season with salt and pepper. Add vegetables if desired, cut into small cubes. Pour the filling into the casserole and cover it loosely with foil. Refrigerate the casserole if making ahead.

The topping:

Have ready a potato ricer or food mill (first choices), a masher, or a fork.

Put the potatoes in a large pot of generously salted cold water and bring to a boil. Cook until the potatoes are tender enough to be pierced easily with the tip of a knife, about 20 minutes; drain them well.

Meanwhile, center a rack in the oven and preheat the oven to 400 degrees F. Line a baking sheet with foil or a silicone baking mat to catch drips.

Warm the milk and cream.

Run the potatoes through the ricer or food mill into a bowl, or mash them well. Using a wooden spoon or spatula, stir in the milk and cream, then blend in the 3 tablespoons butter. Season to taste with salt and pepper.

Spoon the potatoes over the filling in the casserole, spreading them evenly and making sure they reach to the edges of the casserole. Sprinkle the grated Gruyere, Comte or Emmental over the top of the pie, dust with the

Parmesan (if using), and scatter over the bits of butter. Place the dish on the lined baking sheet. Bake for 30 minutes, or until the filling is bubbling and the potatoes have developed a golden crust.

Serving

Bring the *Hachis Parmentier* to the table and spoon out. Add a green salad for a satisfying French meal.

Storing

You can make this dish in stages: the beef can be made up to a day ahead, and the filling can also be prepared ahead and both kept covered in the fridge. You can also assemble the entire dish ahead and keep it chilled for a few hours before baking it (directly from the refrigerator if your casserole can stand the temperature change) — of course, you'll have to bake it a little longer. For leftovers, reheat them in a 350F oven.

֍

from **The Frenchman**

PASCAL WAS PRESSED INTO TELLING his story of abduction and rescue over a not-so-simple lunch of *hachis parmentier,* a sort of delicious shepherd's pie with layers of mashed potatoes and lamb, served with crusty baguettes and olive tapenade. Wine flowed, as is the French way, then came the *crème brulée* for a sweet finish. Jacques told his tale of survival by goat cheese as well. Everyone enjoyed the drama and offered many compliments for the chef.

As they left Merle brought a print-out of *Odette and the Great Fear,* loose pages wrapped in a rubber band. She pressed the stack on Louise and asked her to translate it for Irene.

"Nothing fancy, just in front of the fire some night, tell her the story."

Louise's eyes widened. "You wrote this?"

"There are goats involved," Merle said. "And a hand-some stranger."

Louise pressed it to her chest. "I will do my best, Merle. Thank you for the honor. My mother will love it."

In the car as they buckled themselves in the seat belts and waved to Irene and Louise on the porch, Pascal said, "What a meal, *mon dieu*. She did us such a courtesy. It was like my mother's *cuisine,* full of love and respect. You know what this means. These are your people now." He touched her shoulder. "Our people, blackbird."

"*Our people.* I like the sound of that."

Chapter Three

BLANQUETTE DE VEAU

hat could be more warming and satisfying on a cold winter's night than this delicious French veal stew?

Blanquette de Veau is a classic dish that is served all over France. *Blanquette* is the French term for a ragout of white meat (veal, lamb or poultry) cooked in a white stock or water with aromatic flavorings, without browning in butter — thus keeping it "white." It requires some time, as my friend and fellow francophile Judy Williams discovered when she made it recently. But your effort will be appreciated by friends and family. Thank you, Judy, and thanks to your tasters, Malcolm and Ainsley too.

SERVES 4-6

Ingredients

2-1/2 lbs. veal shoulder (cut into 2-inch cubes)
NOTE: To save time have the butcher cube the veal for

you. You will need to get this from a specialty butcher anyway.

2 carrots
2 leeks
1 small onion
2 garlic cloves, minced
2 small shallots (sliced – keep one half full)
1 celery stalk, sliced
4 cloves
1/2 pound white mushrooms
1/3 pound pearl onions, peeled
4 tbsp white wine (optional)
2 tbsp butter
Salt and pepper, for seasoning

For the bouquet garni:
A bunch of thyme
One bay leaf
A few sprigs of parsley

For the sauce:
A few squeezes of fresh lemon juice
2/3 cup crème fraîche
1/3 cup plain flour
1/4 cup butter
2 egg yolks

Chop the carrots into chunky sticks, coarsely slice the onion, shallots, leeks, celery, and garlic. (Tip to peel pearl onions: trim the root and put in a heat-proof dish, pour boiling water over them and let stand about 4-5 minutes, then plunge into cold water. The skins will peel right off.) Keep half a shallot and stick the cloves in it.

Make a simple bouquet garni with a few sprigs of thyme, parsley and bay leaf (tie with some twine or wrap in cheesecloth).

Blanch the cubed veal in a large Dutch oven in about 8 cups of boiling salted water for 1-2 minutes. Add the onion, shallots, garlic, bouquet garni and all the other vegetables-- except mushrooms and pearl onions but including the half shallot with cloves. Add the wine. Bring to a soft boil for 2 minutes. Season with salt. Cover and cook on a low heat for 1 hour and 15 minutes.

Remove all the meat, bouquet garni, vegetables and set aside. Cover to keep them warm. Strain the broth through a fine-mesh sieve, reserving four cups of broth. Then boil down the broth to 2 cups for the sauce.

In a saucepan melt ¼ c. butter and add 1/3 c. flour, cooking over low heat until smooth and golden to make a roux. Add the 2 cups of stock from the pot and mix well. Pour the roux sauce into the blanquette pot. Mix well with a whisk and cook for 5 minutes on a low heat, until the stew sauce starts to slightly thicken. Return the veal and strained veggies to the pot and simmer about 15 minutes.

. . .

At the same time, sauté the sliced mushrooms and peeled pearl onions in 2 T butter. Drizzle with Lemon juice and add to blanquette.

In a separate, medium bowl combine the crème fraiche, lemon juice, and 2 egg yolks. Add 1 – 2 ladles of blanquette sauce to the bowl – you don't want to curdle the eggs. Stir well, then return the mixture to the blanquette. Warm gently and serve with rice. Garnish with parsley.

NOTES: Two-and-a-half pounds of veal shoulder before trimming was plenty for 6 people. The ancient version of this recipe recommends pasta instead of rice. Sometimes even potatoes are used as a base.

Chapter Four

COQ AU VIN

One of my family's favorite meals, *Coq au Vin* or Chicken in Wine, is a simple, tasty country stew similar to *Boeuf bourguignon* but is made with chicken instead of beef — *bien sûr*— of course.

SERVES 4

Ingredients

  2 tbsp olive oil

  4 ounces (3-4 slices) bacon or pancetta, diced

  1 (3 to 4-pound) chicken, cut in 8ths. Or use precut pieces, boneless or bone-in thighs are good, figure 2 thighs per person.

  Kosher salt and freshly ground black pepper

  Herbes de Provence, to taste

  2 large carrots, cut diagonally in 1-inch pieces

  1 shallot, sliced

1 tsp chopped garlic
1/2 bottle (2 1/2 cups) dry red wine
1 cup chicken stock
10 fresh thyme sprigs
2 tablespoons unsalted butter, divided
1 1/2 tablespoons all-purpose flour
1/2 pound frozen pearl onions (optional)
1/2 pound cremini mushrooms, stems removed and thickly sliced

Preheat the oven to 300 F.

Heat the olive oil in a large Dutch oven. Add the bacon and cook over medium heat for 8 to 10 minutes, until lightly browned. Remove the bacon to a plate with a slotted spoon. Add carrots and shallot to the pot, salt and pepper to taste, and cook for 7 to 8 minutes, stirring. Add garlic and cook for 1 more minute. Remove from the pot.

Liberally salt and pepper the chicken on both sides, adding herbes de Provence. Brown the chicken pieces in batches in a single layer for about 5 minutes, turning to brown evenly. Remove the chicken to the plate with the bacon and continue until all the chicken is done.

Put the bacon, carrots, garlic, and shallot, plus any juices that collected on the plate back into the pot with the chicken pieces. Add the wine, chicken stock, and thyme and bring to a simmer. Cover the pot with a tight fitting lid and place in the oven for about 45 minutes, until the chicken is just not pink. Remove from the oven and place on top of the stove.

Mash 1 tablespoon of butter and the flour together and stir into the stew. Add the frozen onions if using them. Meanwhile, in a medium pan, melt the remaining 1 tablespoon of butter and cook the mushrooms over medium-low heat for 5 to 10 minutes, until browned then add to the pot. Simmer for another 10 minutes.

Serve hot with rice, pasta, or boiled potatoes.

Chapter Five

CHICKEN PAILLARD

A paillard is a piece of meat pounded thin then quickly sautéed. You will need plastic wrap or a large plastic bag, plus a wooden mallet or the handle of a large knife.

This simple dish is very elegant, perfect for Valentine's Day. Merle and Pascal enjoy Chicken Paillard in New York City in **Give Him the Ooh la la**.

SERVES 4

Ingredients

  2 teaspoons lemon zest
  3 tablespoons lemon juice
  2 teaspoons extra virgin olive oil
  1 garlic clove, crushed
  1/2 teaspoon salt, divided
  1/2 teaspoon freshly ground black pepper, divided

4 cups trimmed arugula
4 (6-ounce) skinless, boneless chicken breast halves
Cooking spray
1 cup grape or cherry tomatoes, halved
1/3 cup dry white wine

Combine lemon zest, juice, oil, and garlic in a large bowl. Add 1/4 teaspoon salt and 1/4 teaspoon pepper and arugula; toss well. Refrigerate until needed.

Place chicken breast between 2 sheets of heavy-duty plastic wrap or into a ziplock bag; pound each piece to 1/4-inch thickness using a mallet, knife handle, or small heavy skillet. Sprinkle both sides of chicken with remaining 1/4 teaspoon salt and remaining 1/4 teaspoon pepper.

Heat a large nonstick skillet over medium-high heat. Coat pan with cooking spray. Add chicken, and cook for 4 minutes on each side or until done. Do not overcook. Remove chicken from pan, and keep warm.

Add halved tomatoes and dry white wine to pan. Cook for 2 minutes or until the liquid almost evaporates. Pour sauce and tomatoes over the chicken. Serve with arugula.

૮.

from **Give Him the Ooh la la**

.   .   .

Pascal stood at a table, wearing the same striped shirt from this morning, waving his napkin at her. The hostess saw him too and led her through the white table-cloths and clinking flatware. He kissed her on both cheeks and a third for luck, pulled out her chair, took her coat, and settled her in. It felt good. His manners, after the embarrassing months with ridiculous James, made her feel safe and respected. If that's what manners were for there should be classes.

He looked different, she noticed, smiling. It was that he was smiling, really smiling, looking around the big room with its crowded tables and bustling wait staff.

"It's very French," Merle said, putting her napkin in her lap as the waiter poured water into goblets.

"I've ordered the wine," Pascal said. "They have a nice list."

It appeared just like that, a bottle of red, a Château Margaux, on the arm of young hipster in white. "Are we celebrating?" she asked. That wine was expensive, no matter what year.

He squeezed her hand, silent until the sommelier had finished pouring their glasses and vanished. He picked up his glass, looked in her eyes, and said a simple "*Santé.*" Their glasses clinked.

"Mmmm. Very good." Merle set her glass down. "What's going on?"

"First we order." Heads together, they discussed the menu, talking up the merits of duck confit or warm goat cheese salad, chicken *paillard* or *foie gras*. It all sounded good so they ordered too much, happy with their extravagance.

"All right, we've ordered." Merle turned to him as he refilled her wine glass.

He looked at her expectant face. "I have had a break in the case."

Chapter Six

MAGRET DE CANARD WITH RASPBERRY SAUCE

For a special Christmas dinner in **Give Him the Ooh-la-la,** Merle's boyfriend, Pascal, prepares this fabulous duck dish served all over France. Duck is especially popular in the Aquitaine, the region of southwest France where Merle has her cottage. The addition of raspberry sauce makes it extra special, and Christmas-y.

Magret de Canard is duck breast from the *Mulard* breed of ducks, a cross between the White Pekin and the Muscovy duck. It may be difficult to find in the US. In France, *magret* generally refers specifically to the breast of mulard ducks that have been raised on the *foie gras* plan—that is, force-fed until their livers are obscenely obese. This makes the entire duck rich in flavor.

The recipe serves two, but easily multiplied for a larger group.

Ingredients:
1 Magret de Canard Duck Breast

1 Shallot, chopped
1/2 bottle dry red wine
1/2 cup Crème de Cassis
1 Tablespoon Raspberries
1/4 cup Butter

To make the Raspberry Sauce: Bring the wine to the boil and add the shallots. Boil gently until it has reduced by half. Add the *crème de cassis* and raspberries and reduce again. The sauce should be syrupy. Whisk in the butter.

To make the Duck: Slash the fatty side of the duck breast with a sharp knife in a criss-cross pattern. In a hot heavy sauté pan cook the duck breast fat side down for several minutes until the duck fat is golden and starts to render down. Place in the oven at 400F for 10 - 12 minutes fat side up. This will give you medium rare meat.

Spoon raspberry sauce onto each plate and top with half of the duck breast. Serve hot.

❧

from **Give Him the Ooh la la**

Pascal d'Onscon leafed through a *Paris Match* that was four months old in the consulate reception, trying to be patient. The envoy, whose real purpose at the New York office appeared to be film festivals and pastry shop appearances, was having a second cappuccino with a very attractive divorcée. Annoying but very French.

On the other hand Pascal was feeling rather pleased with the way his Christmas dinner turned out. He had rushed the potatoes and green beans a bit, there was some crunch to the beans but he liked them that way. You never knew how Americans would react to dishes you've been eating your whole life. The Bennetts were amiable people, not surprising since they raised Merle and her sisters. The mother had only winced during the raw oysters, blinking, horrified, as if he'd suggested raw snails. Oh, he should have made snails. That would have really wound her up.

He wasn't entirely happy with the white Bordeaux he'd chosen for the cheese course. No one seemed to care. The *magret de canard* was a bold move. He'd been worried about finding perfect duck breasts. Luck and an internet search had helped with that.

All in all his sisters would be proud. He had sent them both photos from the kitchen and they exclaimed their surprise and pleasure at his efforts to please his special friend. That was what they called Merle. They said she was too old to be called his '*petite amie.*' They didn't approve of her. She was older than they were, they squealed. That made Merle a '*voleur berceau,*' a cradle robber. His sisters had a natural but smothering interest in his love life. They had adored his wife, right up to the day she moved back to Paris with her music instructor.

Chapter Seven

ROSSINI DE CANARD

This is a dish for a special occasion; it is rich in every sense of the word, containing duck, foie gras, and truffles. Merle and Pascal have this treat for a romantic lunch in Périgueux in **The Girl in the Empty Dress.**

SERVES 6

Ingredients

. . .

6 duck tournedos - flattened duck breasts, small
  6 small slices of raw foie gras, fresh or frozen
  1 truffle (fresh or bottled)
  3 cups (approx) extra-fine green beans, fresh or frozen
  6 slices of slightly sweet, soft white or wheat bread
(*pain de mie*)
  2 tbsp chopped shallots
  2 tbsp powdered veal stock, or veal (or veal and duck)
demi-glace
  4 tbsp Madeira
  1 1/2 tbsp butter
  salt
  fresh ground pepper

Let the foie gras come to room temperature. Drain the
truffle if it is bottled and keep the juice. Cut it into six
thin slices. In a small saucepan brown the shallots in the
butter, then add the veal stock or demi-glace, add 2 CUPS
of water, mix and let reduce over low heat for about 15
minutes.

Meanwhile plunge the beans into boiling salted water
and cook for 12 minutes then drain. Toast the slices of
bread. Cut off the crust.

In a heavy skillet, sear the duck tournedos over high
heat for 2 minutes on each side; keep warm. Deglaze the
cooking juices in the pan with Madeira (and optionally
reserved truffle juice.)

Reduce for a few minutes on high heat.

Sear the foie gras pieces on both sides in a nonstick
skillet, 1-1/2 minutes total. Arrange the slices of bread on

each plate, divide the beans between the plates. Place a tournedo on each slice of toast and salt and pepper them.

Top the tournedos with a slice of foie gras, salt, pepper, then a slice of truffle. Surround with a bead of sauce, add more sauce over the top, and serve immediately.

adapted from Pascale Mosnier (*Marie Claire France Cuisine et Vins*)

———————————

• Duck, veal, or veal-and-duck demi-glace, truffles, and *foie gras,* as well as many other French delicacies, are available online through dartagnan.com Williams-Sonoma also stocks veal demi-glace.

• Fresh truffles too rich for your blood? Try the bottled variety or dried porcini mushrooms— rehydrate them in hot water or the veal stock for 15 minutes— and add a little truffle salt instead of regular salt. Not the same effect, but still delicious.

Chapter Eight

LAMB SHANKS WITH ORANGE

*L*amb Shanks— the lower leg of the lamb— are sometimes difficult to find. You may have to order them at your butcher. The meatier the better, but they vary. Use whatever combination of spices that you like: cloves, ginger, star anise, cardamom, and/or cinnamon. A delicious, warming meal that makes the kitchen smell amazing.

SERVES 3-4

Ingredients

    6 lamb shanks
    Sea salt
    Black pepper
    1-2 tbsp olive oil
    1 medium red onion or 2 shallots, diced
    3 cloves garlic, peeled, left whole

1 tbsp whole cloves and/or 3 star anise, 1 stick cinnamon, 1 tbsp shaved fresh ginger

—- OR 2 tsp ground cinnamon, 1 tsp ground clove or ground cardamom or ground ginger

1 navel orange, cut into eighths

1 tsp sugar

2 cups chicken stock

1 cup dry white wine

Preheat oven to 350 degrees. Brown the lamb shanks in a large, heavy pot. Sprinkle with salt and pepper. Turn over, brown other side, then remove from pan to a plate.

Add oil then onion, garlic, spices, and orange sections. Sauté until lightly browned, about five minutes. Add the lamb shanks back into the pan, standing on end. Add stock, wine, and sugar. Bring to boil.

Put the cover on the pot and place in the preheated oven for 1 1/2 to 2 hours. Lamb should be tender and the sauce reduced. Transfer the meat to a platter and serve with sauce from the pot drizzled over them. Arrange orange slices and whole spices over and around them.

Chapter Nine

BEEF CHEEKS IN RED WINE

This delectable French recipe is similar to one I make using simply chuck roast with *quatre épices*: four spices (ground pepper (white, black, or both), cloves, nutmeg and dried ginger) with onions and little else. This recipe adds red wine and carrots, with orange zest to spice things up. This was Francie Bennett's favorite dish in the Sancerre in **The Frenchman.**

Beef cheeks are literally that, the muscle on the cow's jaw used to chew their cud. Thus they can be tough and need a slow braise in wine to become meltingly tender. A slow cooker can also be used for this recipe.

Ingredients
   2 pounds beef cheeks or boneless beef chuck roast
   2 tablespoons extra virgin olive oil
   1 pound onions, coarsely chopped
   1 pound carrots, peeled and cut into two-inch pieces

1 (750-ml) bottle dry red wine
6 to 8 (3- by 1-inch) strips of orange zest

Preheat oven to 350°F.

If using chuck, cut across grain to make 4 pieces. Season with 1 tsp salt and 1/2 tsp pepper. Heat oil in a 4- to 6-quart heavy pot over medium-high heat until it shimmers. Brown beef on all sides, 6 to 10 minutes total. Transfer to a plate.

Add onions, carrots, 3/4 tsp salt, and 1/2 tsp pepper to pot and cook, stirring occasionally, until vegetables are softened, 8 to 10 minutes. Add wine and zest and bring to a boil. Add beef and return to a boil. Cover the pot tightly and braise in oven until meat is very tender, 2 to 4 hours (beef cheeks take longer than chuck). Season with salt and pepper. Serve beef with carrots and sauce.

☙

from **The Frenchman**

THE BISTRO in the *auberge* Francie picked out was the main building on the tiny village street, taking up most of a block. The sun shone bright on the stone facade and the 1950s plastic signage. It looked like it hadn't changed in fifty years, which Francie declared an excellent sign.

The restaurant was packed with men and a few women, many of them in the business of winemaking, or so it appeared. A large table at one end seemed communal, grizzled old men with scarred fingers lined up on either side, feasting on olives and bread. The rest of the room was groups of four or six, serious as they examined the color of wine in their glasses or poured over papers.

The sisters snagged one of the last tables, near a window overlooking a side garden. The flowers were dormant, trampled by sun and rain over the summer. Merle took a seat next to the window though, just for the sunshine. Francie read through the menu like her life depended on picking the best, most exotic local tastes.

After they ordered Sancerre *blanche* and *quenelle de brochet* (pike dumplings) and beef cheeks in red wine— Merle let Francie order for both of them— they sat back and examined the room.

"See anyone you want to strike up a conversation with?" Merle asked quietly. "An English speaker. That narrows the playing field."

"Yeah, none of those vineyard workers, I guess." Francie nodded toward the communal table. She squinted, catching the eye of an attractive man in a blue suit who raised his glass to her. She nodded coyly and looked away. "Does he look British?"

"He looks single, at least for today."

Chapter Ten

COQUILLES SAINT-JACQUES

*C*oquilles Saint-Jacques is a scallops dish named for Saint Jacques (Saint James in English, Santiago in Spanish), one of the original twelve apostles of Jesus, and the patron saint of Spain.

The scallop shell is the symbol of the crusaders of the Order of St. James, which was founded to protect pilgrims headed across France and northern Spain to the Santiago de Compostela or *Saint-Jacques-de-Compostelle* in French. Modern-day pilgrims on the route follow markers shaped like scallop shells, and bring back a shell from the beach to prove they arrived at the sea, just as their fellow pilgrims of the Middle Ages did.

The scallop shell has been associated since the twelfth century with "good works": "the two valves of the shell represent the two precepts of love... namely to love God more than anything and love his next as oneself." The origin of the shell of Santiago de Compostela is probably derived from this ancient symbolism but also refers to several legends: ashes of the saint arrived at Compostela in a shell; a knight rescued from drowning by the intercession of the saint, just as the boat was passing the burial ship from Jerusalem, and came out of the water covered with shells.

This recipe uses six large scallop shells to serve the dish individually. Shells are available online and at specialty kitchen shops. You can also use ramekins.

SERVES 6

Ingredients
8 oz. button mushrooms, minced
6 tbsp. unsalted butter
3 small shallots, minced
2 tbsp. minced parsley
1 tbsp. minced tarragon, plus 6 whole leaves, to garnish
Sea salt and freshly ground black pepper, to taste
3/4 cup dry vermouth
1 bay leaf
6 large sea scallops
2 tbsp. flour
1/2 cup heavy cream
2/3 cup grated Gruyère cheese
1/2 tsp fresh lemon juice

Heat mushrooms, 4 tbsp. butter, and 2/3 of the shallots in a medium saucepan over medium heat; cook until the mixture forms a loose paste, about 25 minutes. Stir parsley and minced tarragon into mushroom mixture; season with salt and pepper. Divide mixture among 6 cleaned scallop shells or ramekins set on a baking sheet.

Bring remaining shallots, vermouth, bay leaf, salt, and 3/4 cup water to a boil in another saucepan over medium heat. Add scallops; cook until barely tender, about 2 minutes. Remove scallops; place one in each shell, over mushrooms. Continue boiling cooking liquid until reduced to 1/2 cup, about 10 minutes; strain.

Heat broiler to high. Melt remaining butter in a small saucepan over medium heat. Add flour; whisk and cook until smooth, about 2 minutes. Add reduced cooking liquid and combine, stirring; cook until thickened, about 8 minutes. Add cheese, juice, salt, and pepper; divide the sauce over scallops.

Broil until browned on top, about 3 minutes; garnish each with a tarragon leaf.

Chapter Eleven

SALMON TARTARE WITH AVOCADO

Tartare de Saumon à la coriandre et sauce Aurore

Merci beaucoup to my friends, Patricia and Laurent Zirotti, from Fleur de Sel, a French bistro in Post Falls, Idaho, for sharing this delicious appetizer or small entrée. Laurent is a James Beard-nominated chef and the couple's restaurant has received many honors.

This dish features raw (that's what 'tartare' means) salmon mixed with herbs and spices and avocado, and is served in the half-peel of the avocado with a classic French sauce. Make sure the salmon is of very good quality and freshness.

SERVES 4

Ingredients

. . .

Sauce Aurore
- ½ cup of mayonnaise good quality
- 1 tablespoon of ketchup
- 1 teaspoon of Cognac or Whiskey

Filling
- 2 avocados
- ¼ red onion finely minced
- ½ bunch of cilantro chopped
- 1 tablespoon of fresh ginger grated
- 1 lime (grated zest and juice)
- 2 tablespoon of capers chopped
- 8 oz of Scottish wild salmon or Alaskan wild king salmon

Instructions

Cut the avocado lengthwise in half and remove the pit. With a spoon remove gently the inside of the avocado keeping the skin in one piece. Mash the avocado in a bowl with a fork or in a mortar.

Make the sauce Aurore by whisking all ingredients together (mayonnaise, ketchup and alcohol.)

In a large bowl mix well the avocado, chopped onion, grated ginger, grated lime zest, lime juice, chopped cilantro, and chopped capers.

Remove skin and pin bones from the salmon. With a sharp knife cut in very small dice the raw salmon and mix it with all other ingredients. Add three-quarters of the sauce Aurore and combine with a spatula. If you feel that the mix is too dry add the rest of the sauce.

With a serving spoon place back the mix in each of the

4 avocado skins, using them as a service support. Place a dollop of the remaining sauce Aurore on each, or dot it artistically onto the plate. Decorate with whole cilantro leaves or other micro greens.

Sit the filled avocado over a salad mix of your choice.

Bon appetit!

Chapter Twelve

MADELEINES À LA HÉLÈNE

These classic French sweet bites are like mini-cakes, baked in special pans that give them the shape of shells, similar to the *coquilles* or scallops. The tea cakes are believed to have first been made by a young maid named Madeleine who was employed by the Duke of Lorraine, the deposed King of Poland, Stanisław Leszczyński, in the late 1700s.

This basic recipe can be adapted with the addition of many flavors, making the madeleine unique to you. See cookbooks on Amazon Pans are available at most kitchen shops. Metal and silicone pans can be used; my friend and madeleine chef Helen recommends the flexible silicone ones for ease in removal.

Madeleines were made famous by Marcel Proust in his seminal work, *In Search Of Lost Time* (*À la recherche du temps perdu*) when he recalled the pleasure of tasting one dipped in tea for the first time:

> No sooner had the warm liquid mixed with the crumbs touched my palate than a shudder ran through me and I stopped, intent upon the extraordinary thing that was happening to me.

Ingredients

5 eggs
1-1/2 sticks (3/4 cup) butter, room temperature
1-1/2 cup sugar
1-1/2 cup flour
1 teaspoon vanilla
zest of one lemon

Instructions

Preheat oven to 325F. Butter madeleine pans (makes about 12)

In the bowl of an electric mixer whip together the eggs and butter until light. Stir in the remaining ingredients.

Cover and chill the batter in the refrigerator for one hour. Spoon into the pans and bake for about 15 minutes, until golden. Cool in the pan for a few minutes, then invert onto a wire rack to cool completely.

Sift with powdered sugar just before serving.

Chapter Thirteen

CHAMPAGNE TRUFFLE OMELET

*L*ooking for a quintessential French brunch dish, or perhaps a super special dinner idea? Look no further than this truffle omelet made with a little Champagne, raclette cheese, and crème fraiche. Merle often orders this omelet with Pascal, at her favorite Malcouziac bistro, *Les Saveurs*.

"Your special omelet gets cold."

It was big enough to feed her for a week. She cut off a piece and hummed with the taste of truffles, woodsy and delicate and unique among mushrooms, dug from the roots of ancient oak trees.

— *Blackbird Fly*

Can't find raclette cheese? Substitute Gruyère, Fontina, or Emmental.

• • •

Ingredients

2 large eggs
1 tablespoon Champagne
1 teaspoon fresh black truffle, grated
Pinch of salt
1 tablespoon crème fraiche
2 tablespoons raclette cheese
1 teaspoon fresh tarragon, lightly chopped
Pinch of kosher salt
1 tablespoon butter

Instructions

In a small bowl, combine the eggs, Champagne, grated truffle, pinch of salt, crème fraiche, cheese, and chopped tarragon. Use a fork to fully blend eggs with all ingredients, whipping for a least a minute or two, until the whites and yolks are blended completely, without stripes of white and yolk.

Over medium-high heat, use a small, 9-inch non-stick pan to melt the butter. Pour egg mixture in at once. Let the first layer of egg set on the bottom and the sides. Keep the heat medium high, pull the sides of the setting egg into the center a few times to let the uncooked egg run underneath and set, rotate pan with your wrist, as most of the egg begins to set and the top is creamy and moist, roll the omelet by tilting the pan forward and let the edges roll over, about 1 minute into cook time. Reduce the heat to medium, and gently flip the omelet once, and let finish cooking 10 to 20 seconds or more, until the surface is set. The inside should be creamy, moist, medium rare. (Cook a few minutes more for medium to firm.)

Serve hot.

Chapter Fourteen

ALIGOT

*T*his classic peasant dish will build up your arm strength as well as warm your toes.

A cross between fondue and mashed potatoes, *Aligot* is a traditional dish from the Aveyron. It is said to have originated in the mountains on the trails to Santiago, where villagers would offer it to pilgrims. Best with a traditional acidic cheese like Tomme d'Auvergne or a Cantal.

SERVES 6– 8

Ingredients

2 pounds Yukon Gold potatoes, peeled and cut into quarters

3/4 teaspoon salt

1/8 teaspoon ground white pepper

4 tablespoons butter

1/4 cup crème fraîche (or 1/8 cup sour cream and 1/8 cup heavy cream)

1 clove garlic, lightly crushed

3 cups Tomme de l'Aveyron, Laguoile, d'Aubrac, or young Cantal cheese, cut into thin slices. Substitute white cheddar or cheddar cheese curds in a pinch.

Boil potatoes in cold, salted water for 20 minutes until tender. Do not overcook. Drain.

Mash potatoes using a hand potato ricer or a rotating potato *moulinette* (food mill) with a hand crank. Add salt, white pepper, and butter. Mix well for 2 or 3 minutes until fluffy. Set back into the pan.

In a saucepan over medium heat, bring crème fraîche and garlic to steaming. Do not boil.

Remove the garlic and pour hot crème fraîche over the potatoes and transfer too pan of potatoes to the stove over low heat. Beat the crème fraîche into the potatoes with a wooden spoon until they start to turn glossy. Raise heat to medium and beat in the grated cheese a 1/2 cup at a time. Continue mixing the potatoes and cheese until it forms a smooth, velvety texture. This should take about ten minutes, during which you will get a good upper body workout. When ready, lifting the spoon should create stretchy strings of cheesy potatoes.

Serve immediately on warmed plates.

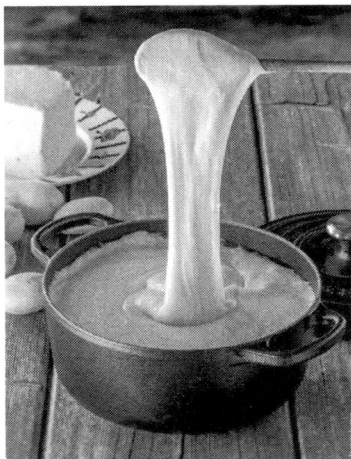

Aligot

Chapter Fifteen

TARTIFLETTE

*T*his potato and cheese casserole is a testament to the French love of *fromage*. Maybe a little green salad to add some color but enough on its own to warm all on a winter night.

SERVES 4— 5

Ingredients

  2-1/2 pounds of russet potatoes, about 6 medium
  1 large onion, thinly sliced
  1/2 pound pancetta (or slab bacon) diced
  1 clove of garlic
  1 cup of dry white wine
  1 pound Reblonchon type cheese, a soft cow's milk cheese such as Le Delice de Jura (In the US a good substitute is Raclette.)

. . .

Wash and cut the potatoes into thick slices (but don't peel) and then boil in salted water until just beginning to feel tender.

In a large frying pan, sauté the pancetta lightly, not browning, then remove them from the pan and sauté the onions in the same pan until soft, and then remove to a plate.

Add some butter to the pan (if necessary) and add the cooked, drained potatoes and sauté for five minutes. Add the onions, pancetta, crushed garlic and wine and continue cooking for about five minutes (until the wine has evaporated).

Pour half the potato mixture into an oven dish. Cut the round of cheese into two disks the same thickness, and then place one on top of potato mixture. Repeat with the rest of the potato mixture and another disk of cheese. Bake in a 350F oven for about twenty minutes, until the cheese is golden brown and bubbling. Serve and enjoy its melty deliciousness.

Adapted from FrenchVillageDiaries.com
Thank you, Jacqui.

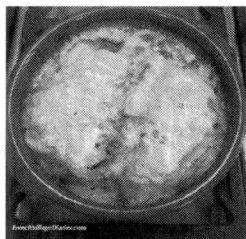

Tartiflette

Chapter Sixteen

CÉLERI RÉMOULADE

Celeriac, or celery root— *céleri* in French— is a bit of a mystery to many Americans. It's simply the root of the celery, the stalks of which we usually eat. It's round, and white after peeling, and surprisingly tasty. Yes, it tastes like celery! Refreshingly light and crunchy. This side salad, similar to cole slaw, is often found in delis in France.

Ingredients
    1 medium celery root, peeled
    2 tbsp lemon juice
    1/3 cup mayonnaise
    1 tbsp. Dijon mustard
    salt and pepper to taste
    1 tbsp snipped chives (optional)

Instructions
    Grate a medium-sized peeled celery root, around 12

oz. or the size of large softball. Toss with lemon juice immediately to keep it fresh.

Whisk together mayonnaise, Dijon mustard, salt, pepper, and snipped chives.

Add the dressing to the grated celery root and toss to coat. Add more pepper to taste.

Makes a refreshing starter or salad course.

Chapter Seventeen

CELERY ROOT MASH WITH POACHED EGGS

$\mathcal{C}$elery root is not common in the US as we seem to prefer the stalks alone. But the root, which tastes similar to the stalks, is tasty as well. It is easy to peel and can be grated in the food processor or food mill.

Ingredients
1 celery root, peeled
1 to 1 1/2 sticks of butter
celery leaves from one bunch
6 eggs
salt
slivers of truffle (optional)

Instructions
Cube and boil the celery root in salted water. When tender, drain well. Mash with the butter. Use as much as looks tasty, don't be shy. Chop the celery leaves and stir into the mash.

Put the mash into a baking dish and make 6 indentations. Fill each one with an egg. (Alternately make them separately in ramekins, see photo.) Season each egg with a bit of salt and top with a dot of butter.

Bake in a 475F oven until the eggs set but the yolks are still runny, about 8-9 minutes.

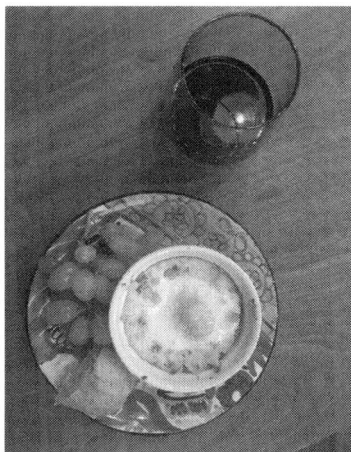

Chapter Eighteen

FRENCH ONION SOUP

*S*oupe à l'Oignon Gratinée

A classic all over the world. Made from scratch is always best. Yum. You will need 6 ovenproof ramekins or crocks.

Makes 6 servings or 4 as a main dish

Ingredients

    4 tablespoons unsalted butter (1/2 stick)
    2 pounds yellow onions, thinly sliced
    3 fresh thyme sprigs
    1 bay leaf
    1 teaspoon kosher salt, plus more to taste
    2 teaspoons all-purpose flour
    3/4 cup dry white wine
    4 cups beef broth

1 1/2 cups water
Freshly ground black pepper, to taste
6 (1/2-inch) slices from a baguette
8 oz Gruyère cheese, grated
2 tablespoons finely grated Parmesan cheese (optional)

Instructions

Melt the butter in a large Dutch oven or heavy soup pot over low heat. Add the onions, thyme, bay leaf, and measured salt. Slowly cook down the onions, stirring frequently until the onions are very soft and a deep golden brown, about 45 minutes. Reduce heat if overcooking. Add the flour, stir well, and cook, stirring, for 1 minute. Add the wine and simmer, stirring, for 2 minutes. Add the broth and water, bring it to a boil, and simmer gently, stirring occasionally, for 30 minutes. Taste and add salt and pepper to taste.

Heat oven (or toaster oven) to 350°F. Arrange the baguette slices in a single layer on a baking sheet and toast on middle rack for 5 minutes. Turn the slices over and toast an additional 5 minutes.

Turn on the broiler and arrange the crocks or ramekins on a rimmed baking sheet or in a shallow baking pan.

When the soup is finished, remove bay leaf and thyme

sprigs and discard them. Ladle the soup evenly among the crocks, then top each with a baguette toast. Sprinkle the crocks with the shredded Gruyère and grated Parmesan.

Place under the broiler, about 4 to 5 inches from the heat, until the cheese is melted and bubbly, about 2 minutes.

Serve immediately.

Chapter Nineteen

WARM GOAT CHEESE SALAD

*S*alade Chèvre Chaud

Have I mentioned I love goat cheese? All flavors: truffled, lemon, herb, plain. Whenever I find a warm goat cheese salad on a menu I usually go for it. Unfortunately at bistros and cafes, even in France, they range from the sublime to the mediocre to the "what did I order again?" So make them the way you like them at home! This is a classic recipe of crumb-crusted goat cheese rounds over simple greens.

SERVES 4

Ingredients
    8 oz goat cheese log (fresh chèvre-style goat cheese)
    1/2 cup panko or bread crumbs (chilled)

1 tbsp vegetable or olive oil

6 cups tender salad greens

3 tablespoons extra virgin olive oil

1 tablespoon red wine vinegar

1/4 teaspoon ground mustard

1 dash flaky sea salt

1 dash freshly ground black pepper

Preheat oven to 375 F. Cut the goat cheese crosswise into 8 to 10 rounds.

Put the panko or bread crumbs into a shallow bowl. Mix the 1 tbsp vegetable or olive oil into the panko. Press the goat cheese rounds into the panko, covering thoroughly on both sides and the edges as well. Set the coated goat cheese on a baking sheet or platter. Place the platter in the freezer for 15 to 30 minutes to set before cooking.

In a large salad bowl, whisk together the 3 tbsp olive oil, vinegar, and mustard. Add salt and pepper to taste and add washed and drained lettuce to the bowl. Toss the salad, then divide it between 4 plates.

Remove the goat cheese from the freezer. Bake the goat cheese croutes on a baking sheet until browned, about 15 minutes. Top each salad with 2 or 3 goat cheese croutes and serve immediately.

Chapter Twenty

SPINACH AND GOAT CHEESE QUICHE

I adore goat cheese (as I already mentioned!) And also quiche! This tasty quiche is popular all over France but most common in the southwest where Rocamadour goat cheese comes from. You can use any fresh goat cheese in this quiche.

Ingredients

1 ready-made pie crust, in roll or in a pan

2 pounds fresh spinach

1 leek finely chopped

4-6 pieces of thin sliced bacon, diced

1 teaspoon butter

3 ounces Rocamadour (or other) fresh goat cheese, the size of a "crottin"

3 eggs

1 1/4 cups half & half (or heavy cream if you like)

2/3 cup grated gruyère cheese

salt and pepper to taste

. . .

Wash the spinach well and roughly chop then place it in a large colander to drain. Put the cut washed spinach it in a large saucepan and cook the spinach until it is wilted – you will not need to add water when cooking as the water clinging to the washed spinach will be sufficient. When the spinach is cooked return it to the colander and let it drain for an hour.

Preheat the oven to 350 F. Grease a pie or quiche dish with butter, then line with pie crust, trimming the edges. Prick the crust all over with a fork and line with a layer of baking paper. Half fill with rice or baking beans or pie weights to keep the crust flat and cook for 10 minutes. Remove from the oven. Remove weights/beans/rice and paper.

Meanwhile in a large frying pan cook the leeks in a small amount of butter on low heat until they start to soften and add the bacon and cook until the leeks are soft, then add the spinach to the mixture and stir.

In a separate bowl beat the eggs together and then add the half & half or cream, Gruyère cheese, salt and pepper.

Spread the spinach mixture into the pie crust and then pour the egg mixture over the it. Place sliced disks of goat cheese over the top. Bake for 30 to 40 minutes until browned and liquids have set. Remove from oven and let it set for five or ten more minutes, then cut and serve warm.

Chapter Twenty-One

GOUGÈRES

A *gougère* is a baked savory, flaky roll made of *choux* dough (a light pastry made without sugar) and mixed with cheese. *Gougères* are said to come from Burgundy, particularly the town of Tonnerre.

Gougères can be made as small, appetizer-size pastries, or larger, dinner-size ones, or made into a ring. In Burgundy, they are often served cold when tasting wine in cellars, but are also served warm as an appetizer.

These French delicacies are a bit of a test of your fortitude as a chef. The best gougères are airy and light, golden brown with a hollow center.

Ingredients

6 tablespoons (3⁄4 stick) unsalted butter, cut into pieces

3⁄4 teaspoon kosher salt

Pinch of nutmeg

1-1⁄4 cups all-purpose flour

4 large eggs

6 ounces (1 1⁄2 cups) grated Comté or Gruyère cheese

1⁄2 teaspoon freshly ground black pepper

1 large egg yolk

Instructions

Preheat oven to 400°F.

Bring butter, salt, nutmeg, and 1 cup water to a boil in a medium saucepan, stirring until butter is melted. Remove from heat, add flour, and stir to combine.

Cook mixture over medium heat, stirring vigorously with a wooden spoon, until mixture pulls away from sides of pan and forms a ball, about 2 minutes. Continue to cook, stirring vigorously, until a dry film forms on bottom and sides of pan and dough is no longer sticky, about 2 minutes longer.

Remove pan from heat and let dough cool slightly, about 2 minutes. Mix in whole eggs one at a time, incorporating each one fully between additions. Mix in cheese and pepper.

Scrape dough into a piping bag fitted with a 1⁄2" round tip (alternatively, use a plastic bag with a 1⁄2" opening cut diagonally from one corner). Pipe 1" rounds about 2" apart onto 2 parchment-lined baking sheets. Whisk egg yolk and 1 tsp. water in a small bowl; brush rounds with egg wash.

Bake *gougères* until puffed and golden and dry in the center (they should sound hollow when tapped), 20–25 minutes.

Chapter Twenty-Two

GREEN OLIVE AND BASIL TAPENADE

This spread is delicious in the summer for a picnic on slices of baguette.

Ingredients

8 oz green olives stuffed with anchovies (or plain pitted green olives and a squirt of anchovy paste)

2 garlic gloves, crushed

Half a handful of fresh basil, torn

2 slices stale bread, wetted then squeezed dry

2 - 3 oz extra virgin olive oil

1-2 tsp white wine vinegar (optional)

Salted crackers, toast, or lettuce leaves to serve

Put olives, garlic, basil and bread into a food processor and whizz for 30 seconds. With machine running drizzle in as much olive oil as needed for a pleasant texture. Add vinegar to taste, whizz again, and serve with crackers, toasts, or lettuce leaves.

Chapter Twenty-Three

QUATRE QUARTS

The name **'Quatre Quarts'** translates as four fourths, to make up one whole, in this case one pound cake.

The Quatre Quarts cake is something French housewives throw together for afternoon tea, or in case a neighbor drops by. It would be impolite not to have something to serve. The ingredients here are so simple: eggs, butter, sugar, and flour, that anyone can keep them on hand. Merle Bennett is served this cake on her first visit to Malcouziac, the fictional village in the Dordogne in **Blackbird Fly.**

Ingredients

3 large eggs
1-1/4 cups all-purpose flour
3/4 cup sugar
3/4 cup butter, salted or unsalted (1 1/2 sticks)

. . .

Pour the sugar in a bowl. Add the melted butter and blend it in with a wooden spoon until smooth. Separate the egg yolks from the whites. Set the whites aside. Add the egg yolks to the sugar-butter mix. Stir well. The more you beat, the lighter the cake. Slowly add the sifted flour and incorporate it gradually. Add some salt (up to a whole teaspoon) if you're using unsalted butter only, and set aside. Add a pinch of salt to the egg whites and beat until stiff. If the egg whites have been beaten enough you should be able to flip the bowl upside down without anything dropping out— in other words, very stiff peaks.

Incorporate the egg whites to the batter, a big spoonful at a time, carefully making under-and-over motions until evenly blended. The foam of the meringue should stay intact. This is important in getting a fluffy cake. Pour the batter in a buttered 9-inch round metallic cake pan.

Bake at 350F for about 45 minutes or until golden and a knife comes out clean from the center.

☙

from **Blackbird Fly**

MADAME SUCHET'S PEA GREEN DOOR opened in a whoosh. Merle handed her a bouquet of red and pink roses in a vase. Madame sat her visitor down, insisting on slices of *quatre quarts,* the ubiquitous pound cake. When she could wait no more, Merle interrupted a treatise on roses.

"*Excusez-moi, madame.* I have a question."

Madame Suchet sat down in a yellow print chair. Merle asked, in French, "Did you know a young girl in the forties named Dominique Redier?"

"*Ici? Dans la ville?*"

"*Oui.*"

Yes, here in the village. Her brown eyes flicked to the window. She arranged her hands, took a deep breath and blew it out. Would she talk, that was what she was asking herself. Should she? Her eyes grazed Merle, then back to the window. A minute passed. Merle ate a bite of pound cake and silently begged for trust, for help. Then the older woman cleared her throat.

"She was two or three years younger than me. A pretty girl, a blond. I didn't know her well."

Merle felt her breath leaving her. Finally, someone was talking.

Chapter Twenty-Four

CHERRY CLAFOUTIS

*W*hat to do with all those cherries in the spring? This classic pie comes to the rescue. The *clafoutis* comes from the Limousin region of France, and while black cherries are traditional, there are numerous variations using other fruits, including red cherries, plums, prunes, apples, pears, cranberries or blackberries. The name derives from Occitan, the language of southern France. *Clafotís*, from the verb *clafir*, means "to fill." As in, fill that pie plate with cherries and sweet batter.

Ingredients

   20 oz fresh sweet cherries, stemmed and pitted
   2 tbsp butter, melted
   4 eggs
   1 cup milk
   3/4 cup flour
   1/4 tsp salt
   1/2 cup sugar
   1/2 tsp almond extract
   1/2 tsp vanilla extract
   powdered sugar for dusting

Instructions

Preheat the oven to 350F. Grease a round 10 inch baking/pie dish with butter. Dust with about 2 tbsp of sugar.

   Arrange the cherries in a single layer; set aside until you prepare the batter.

   In the bowl of an electric mixer mix eggs with remaining sugar and salt. Stir in flour. Add milk, vanilla extract, almond extract and mix well until well blended. Add melted butter and stir to combine until similar to the texture of crepes batter. Pour the mixture over the cherries.

   Bake for about 25-30 minutes until golden brown. Cool on a rack for few minutes. Sprinkle with powdered sugar before serving.

Chapter Twenty-Five

KIR, AND KIR ROYALE

A Kir is a delicious aperitif using any white wine mixed with a splash of liqueur. In France you can get a wide variety, from violet liqueur to crème de cassis, a dark concoction made from blackcurrants— which is more traditional. Also traditional is using the white wine called Aligoté, the original grape variety planted by monks to first make wine centuries ago in Burgundy. It was a little harsh so the addition of a drop of liqueur made it more palatable. Or as they say in France— *buvable* (drinkable).

Kir
Mix 1 part Crème de Cassis with 5 parts White Wine.

Kir Royale
Mix 1 part Crème de Cassis with 5 parts Champagne.

The fancy way to serve a Kir is to pour in the wine or champagne then trail the liqueur down the inside of the flute so it settles in the bottom. The addition of a blackberry, a raspberry or some other berry makes a Kir Royale very special.

from **Blame it on Paris**

They spread out a tablecloth he pulled from the bag, sat on it, and popped open a bottle of champagne. He'd even brought flutes. He made cuts into the sides of strawberries with a pocket knife then hung them on the rims of the glasses. He poured the bubbly, brought out cheese and olives, dabbed her chin with a paper napkin.

"You thought of everything, Dylan Hardy," she said, sipping champagne as a breeze blew another snow shower of pink over them. A petal landed in her champagne.

AFTERWORD

I hope you get to try a new French recipe and have enjoyed reading this little cookbook. It's been fun to revisit the food mentioned in the Bennett Sisters mysteries, and test out new recipes. I raise a glass to you, dear readers! *Bon appetit*!

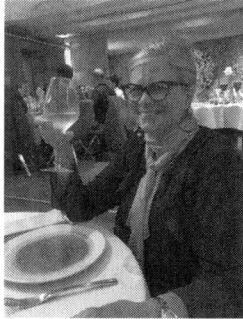

Santé! To your health.

JOIN THE NEWSLETTER LIST

Like to get news about books, deals, and giveaways?

Join the newsletter list and stay up-to-date on all the good stuff!

CLICK HERE

THE BENNETT SISTERS MYSTERIES

Blackbird Fly
The Girl in the Empty Dress
Give Him the Ooh la la
The Things We Said Today
The Frenchman
Odette and the Great Fear
Blame it on Paris

BUY A BOX SET

The Bennett Sisters Mysteries Vol 1-4

The Bennett Sisters Mysteries Vol 1-2
The Bennett Sisters Mysteries Vol 3-4

What are people saying about the Bennett Sisters Mysteries? *Things like…*

Put this in your TBR (to be read) pile! I felt like I trav-

eled to France and I didn't have to leave my couch! [Black-
bird Fly]

A time in the French country side. As always Lise
McClendon delivers. These two books are well written,
leaving you with the feeling that you've been right there
with the characters in the book. The descriptions of the
heat and tastes of French food and the garden leave you
feeling like you took part in the story. [Volume 1 & 2]

Five Stars Love her characters, only problem is when I
finish. I want more! [Things We Said Today]

Amazing I absolutely love the mystery and mystique
of Merle and Pascal in France. The French language is a
joy to read. The author brings her characters to life so
easily. [Volume 1 & 2]

A New Year's Eve celebration for the books!!! I really
enjoyed this book the best out of the ones I have read.
There is so much going on in it that it is hilarious at times,
then sometimes it hits close to Merle Bennett's deceased
husband's family. Not everything is wonderful during this
New Year's Eve celebration, and not everyone is who they
appear to be. A great story! [Give Him the Ooh-la-la]

Great Series!!! Oh how I love this series! I've read all
the books (except for the one about Odette) and really
enjoyed them! Blackbird Fly lured me in and The
Frenchman clinched it! I want more. [The Frenchman]

Love all the Bennett sisters You watch Merle begin to
make a life in France and recover from loss and find new
love. Even her sisters succumb to the magic of France!
Love the character development and find Pascal to be
soooo romantic! Adventure abounds from one book to the
next. I have moved on to the rest of the series and believe
me, you will not be disappointed in what lies ahead for
these sisters! [Volume 1-4]

What can I say? This book has so much going on, but I loved every minute of it. This is one of those books that you just can't put down. The Bennett sisters are a mixed bag of personalities that you both love and hate, who experience hardship, love, failures, and triumphs, and fight like only sisters can do. There is a little bit of mystery, intrigue, humor, and romance on each page. With a well-written storyline, engaging characters, and the background setting of Paris, this is a must-read book. [Blame it on Paris]

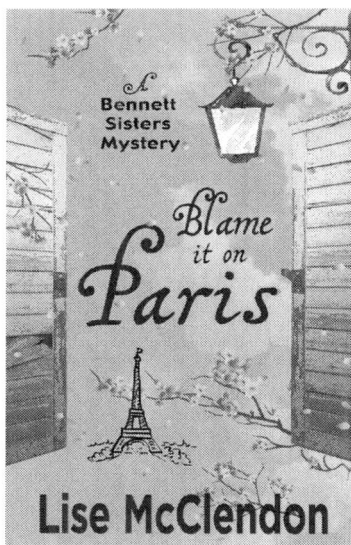

ACKNOWLEDGMENTS

Thank you to all my friends and colleagues who recommended, tested, and shared recipes with me. Kipp, Judy, Jacqui, Helen, Susanna, Laurent, Patricia, and many more: here's to delicious eating wherever we are, and again, *merci*.

LOVE AUDIOBOOKS?

Join Audible and get two free audiobooks. The Bennett
Sisters Mysteries are all available on audio,
on Audible and iTunes.

THE BENNETT SISTERS ON AUDIBLE

THE BENNETT SISTERS ON ITUNES

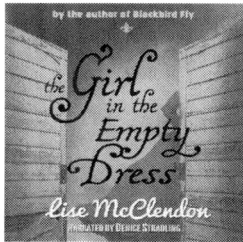

ABOUT THE AUTHOR

Lise McClendon is the author of numerous novels of crime and suspense. Her bestselling Bennett Sisters Mysteries is now in its seventh installment. When not writing about foreign lands and delicious food and dastardly criminals, Lise lives in Montana with her husband. She enjoys fly fishing, hiking, picking raspberries in the summer, and cross-country skiing in the winter. She has served on the national boards of directors of Mystery Writers of America and the International Association of Crime Writers/North America, as well as the faculty of the Jackson Hole Writers Conference. She loves to hear from readers. Follow her on Instagram to see photos of France and more.

This is her first cookbook, made for faithful fans and subscribers to the newsletter. Join us here.

www.lisemcclendon.com

Printed in Great Britain
by Amazon